How Do Insects Protect Themselves?

Megan Kopp

Crabtree Publishing Company

www.crabtreebooks.com

Author
Megan Kopp

Publishing plan research and development
Reagan Miller

Editor
Shirley Duke

Proofreader and indexer
Crystal Sikkens

Design
Samara Parent

Photo research
Tammy McGarr

Prepress technician
Tammy McGarr

Print and production coordinator
Margaret Amy Salter

Photographs
Thinkstock: pgs 4, 6, 7 (top left and right), 8 (top), 12, 19, 21

All other images are from Shutterstock

Library and Archives Canada Cataloguing in Publication

Kopp, Megan, author
       How do insects protect themselves? / Megan Kopp.

(Insects close-up)
Includes index.
Issued in print and electronic formats.
ISBN 978-0-7787-1971-7 (bound).--ISBN 978-0-7787-1975-5 (pbk.).--
ISBN 978-1-4271-9037-6 (pdf).--ISBN 978-1-4271-9033-8 (html)

       1. Insects--Behavior--Juvenile literature. I. Title.

QL467.2.K673 2015   j595.7   C2014-907835-8
                                                              C2014-907836-6

Library of Congress Cataloging-in-Publication Data

Kopp, Megan, author.
 How do insects protect themselves / Megan Kopp.
    pages cm. -- (Insects close-up)
 Includes index.
 ISBN 978-0-7787-1971-7 (reinforced library binding) --
 ISBN 978-0-7787-1975-5 (pbk.) -- ISBN 978-1-4271-9037-6 (electronic pdf) --
 ISBN 978-1-4271-9033-8 (electronic html)
 1. Insects--Defenses--Juvenile literature. 2. Insects--Behavior--Juvenile litera-
ture. 3. Animal defenses--Juvenile literature. I. Title.

 QL467.2.K67 2015
 595.7--dc23
                                 2014045636

Crabtree Publishing Company

Printed in Canada/042015/BF20150203

www.crabtreebooks.com   1-800-387-7650

Published in Canada
Crabtree Publishing
616 Welland Ave.
St. Catharines, Ontario
L2M 5V6

Published in the United States
Crabtree Publishing
PMB 59051
350 Fifth Avenue, 59th Floor
New York, New York 10118

Published in the United Kingdom
Crabtree Publishing
Maritime House
Basin Road North, Hove
BN41 1WR

Published in Australia
Crabtree Publishing
3 Charles Street
Coburg North
VIC 3058

Contents

What are insects?

Insects are animals called **invertebrates**. Invertebrates are animals without backbones. Insects have an **exoskeleton** that protects them. This is a hard shell that covers their body. Insects are the largest group of animals in the world.

Rhinoceros beetles have an odd-shaped exoskeleton. They have horns on their heads.

All kinds of parts

All insects have three parts to their bodies. These are the head, **thorax**, and **abdomen**. They have six legs attached to the thorax. Most insects also have four wings attached to the middle section of their bodies. Insects have two **antennae** on their heads. Insects can be many different shapes and sizes. They also come in many colors.

head

thorax

abdomen

All insects have three body parts and six legs. Spiders and ticks have two body parts and eight legs.

What are predators?

All animals need to eat in order to survive. Some animals hunt other animals for food. They are called **predators**. The animals predators hunt are called **prey**. There are many different animals that eat insects. Birds, bats, and frogs are insect predators. Many bigger insects like to eat smaller insects, too.

Praying mantises eat many different kinds of insects.

Spiders are not insects, but they do eat them.

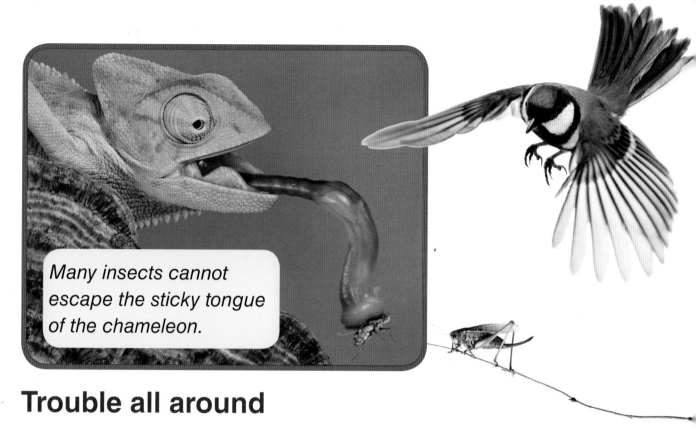

Many insects cannot escape the sticky tongue of the chameleon.

Trouble all around

Insects need to protect themselves in order to survive. Some predators swoop down from the sky. Others can see well in the dark and hunt at night. Insects need to learn where to hide in order to keep away from predators, or they might become prey.

How do insects sense danger?

Sensing danger before it is too late is key to staying alive. Some insects have super senses. They can see, hear, smell, and even feel danger approaching. Some insects, such as flies, have super eyesight.

Cockroaches sense movement in the air with their antennae. Some insects also release **chemicals** into the air. This is a warning to others of possible trouble.

Male Madagascar hissing cockroaches use their antennae to find females by smell.

Super sonic save

Tiger moths are prey for bats.
Bats use **echoes** to find their prey.
Tiger moths sense the danger
and send out fake echoes to
throw off the predator.

What do you think?

What senses do you use
to avoid danger?
How are they similar
to insect senses?

Unlike other tiger moths, Jersey tiger
moths are active during the day.
They use bright colors and patterns
to warn off predators.

Ouch, that hurts!

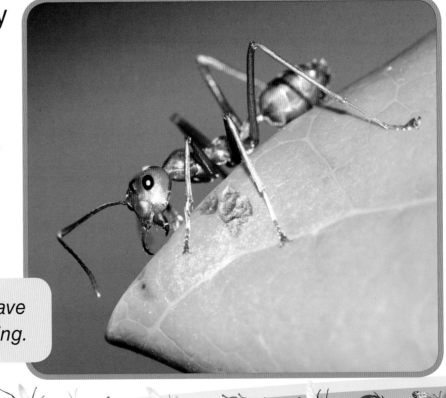

Have you ever been stung by a wasp or bee? It hurts. Some insects bite and sting to keep predators away. Ants and many other insects have nasty bites. Wasps, honeybees, and bumblebees all sting. So do some caterpillars. Many stinging insects are brightly colored. This lets predators know to keep away!

Red ants have a painful sting.

Not all stingers are the same

Stingers are found only on female insects. The stinger sends poison into the predator. Honeybees have hooked stingers. When they sting, the hook stays in the animal or person. Then the bee dies. Wasps and bumblebees don't have barbed stingers. They can sting more than once.

What do you think?

Why is stinging a good defense? If something stings you, do you hang around or get away?

wasp stinger

honeybee stinger

Both wasps and bees will sting if threatened.

11

Can you see me now?

Insects protect themselves from predators in many different ways. Some insects hide in plain sight! These insects **disguise** themselves so that they blend in with their surroundings. This is called **camouflage**.
The Javanese leaf insect looks like a leaf.
What do you think stick insects look like?

Stick insects are often called walking sticks.

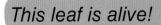

This leaf is alive!

Nothing to see here

Many insects are colored and marked with different patterns. This is called **protective coloring**. It makes them look like their **environment**. It can also make them look like something that a predator would not want to eat. Some moths look like tree bark. Some beetles fall to the ground and look like clumps of dirt.

What do you think?

How do camouflage and protective coloring help protect insects?

Camouflage makes this brown moth hard to see.

Smelly save!

Many insects release a bad-smelling chemical to protect themselves when threatened. The smell is so bad that predators do not attack. Some insects release the chemical as gas. The bombardier beetle lets out a puff of gas from the rear of its body. The gas bothers the predator and it leaves.

Bombardier beetles fight off birds and frogs with gas.

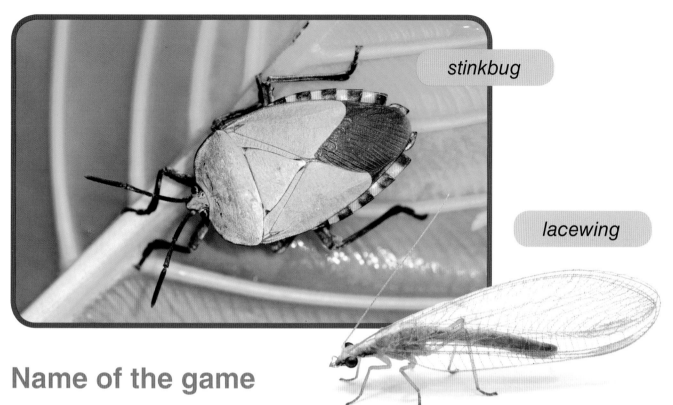

stinkbug

lacewing

Name of the game

Stink bugs get their names because they release a stinky liquid when under attack. This liquid comes from the underside of the insect. It is the stink bugs main defense. Lacewings and broad-headed bugs also use this smelly defense.

Looks can fool you!

Looking dangerous helps protect insects that are not. Some insects look like stinging insects. The hoverfly has yellow stripes on its dark body. It looks like a bumblebee. The hoverfly does not have a stinger. Its color is enough to keep most predators away. Viceroy butterflies look like monarch butterflies. Viceroys are tasty to birds, but monarchs taste bad!

Viceroy butterfly

Monarch butterfly

Looking like something else is a good defense.

The eyes have it

Many species of moths have fake eyespots on their wings. The eyespots are hidden when the moths are resting. When a predator attacks, the moth spreads its wings. Two big eyes appear. The predator thinks that its prey is much bigger and thinks twice about attacking. The moth can then escape.

eyespots

What do you think?

Some insects look like their surroundings instead of other insects. What is this called?

A colorful warning!

Bright colors, such as red, orange, and black, warn predators that something tastes bad. Milkweed bugs have few predators. They eat milkweed plants. The bad tasting sap flavors their bodies. Monarch butterflies lay their eggs on milkweed. Their **larva**, or caterpillars, feed on the plant. Their color says, "Don't eat me!"

monarch caterpiller

Young milkweed bugs are usually found in small groups on milkweed plants.

Stay away

Many ladybugs are brightly colored. If their coloring does not scare away predators, they can release a yellow liquid from their legs that smells. Ladybugs can even play dead if a predator ignores their warnings.

Ladybugs are predators, too. They eat aphids.

Run!

What do you do if you are in a dangerous situation? Most people get away quickly. That is what many insects do! They run, fly, scurry, or hop away from danger. They need to be able to get away from predators quickly in order to keep themselves safe.

Some insects, such as cockroaches, scurry into places where predators can't go.

Eyes on you

Flies have huge eyes. They allow the fly to see in a full circle around itself. As soon as danger comes into view, the fly takes off. Flies react to danger quicker than you can blink! Cockroaches react just as fast to changes in air flow. They scurry away instantly and hide in tiny spaces.

What do you think?

What other insect uses "eyes" to help it stay safe?

21

Super bug

Review the information in this book on how different insects protect themselves. On a separate piece of paper, list the defenses the insects in this chart use to keep themselves safe from predators.

Insect	Defenses
hoverfly	
leaf mantis	
ladybug	
cockroach	
honeybee	
stink bug	

Learning more

Books

Kalman, Bobbie & Rebecca Sjonger. *Insect Defenses (The World of Insects)*. Crabtree Publishing Company, 2006.

Markle, Sandra. *Stick Insects: Masters of Defense.* Lerner Publications, 2008.

Schlitt, Christine. *Perfectly Hidden: The Animal Kingdom's Fascinating Camouflage.* Sky Pony Press, 2013.

Websites

Insect Survival Strategies: Staying Alive in a Bug's World
www.uta.edu/biology/3341/Insect%20Survival%20Strategies.pdf

Ducksters: Stick Bugs
www.ducksters.com/animals/stick_bug.php

Just Kids Game: Build a Bug
http://justkidsgames.com/play.php?BuildABug

23

Words to know

Note: Some **boldfaced** words are defined where they appear in the book.

abdomen (AB-doh-muhn) noun The rear section of an insect's body

antennae (an-TEN-ee) noun Feelers that help insects sense the world around them

camouflage (KAM-uh-flahzh) noun A disguise or natural coloring that allows insects to hide by making them look like their surroundings

chemicals (KEM-i-kuh ls) noun Substances that make up all materials, such as a liquid or gas from a bug

disguise (dis-GIZE) noun A way of dressing or behaving to hide identity

echo (EK-oh) noun A sound that repeats as it bounces back from a surface

environment (en-VYE-ruhn-muhnt) noun The natural surroundings of living things

larva (LAHR-vah) noun A baby insect that hatches from an egg

predators (PRED-uh-ters) noun Animals that hunt other animals for food

prey (prey) noun Animals that are hunted by other animals as food

thorax (THOR-aks) noun The middle section of an insect's body

A noun is a person, place, or thing.

Index